Native American Prehistory

BIBLIOGRAPHICAL SERIES

*The Newberry Library Center
for the History of the American Indian*

General Editor
Francis Jennings
William R. Swagerty, Assistant Editor

The Center is Supported by Grants from

The National Endowment for the Humanities
The Ford Foundation
The W. Clement and Jessie V. Stone Foundation
The Woods Charitable Fund, Inc.
Mr. Gaylord Donnelley

Native American Prehistory

A Critical Bibliography

DEAN R. SNOW

Published for the Newberry Library

Indiana University Press

BLOOMINGTON AND LONDON

Manufactured in the United States of America

Library of Congress Cataloging in Publication Data

Snow, Dean R   1940–
Native American Prehistory

(The Newberry Library Center for the History of the American Indian bibliographical series)
    Includes index.
    1. Indians of North America—Antiquities—Bibliography. I. Title. II. Series: Bibliographical series.
Z1208.N6S67 [E77.9]   016.97'004'97   79–2168
ISBN 0–253–33498–5 pbk.   1 2 3 4 5 83 82 81 80 79

CONTENTS

AUTHOR'S PREFACE

Native Americans have inhabited this continent since well before the end of the last great glaciation, probably about 27,000 years. Yet we have written records for fewer than the past 600. Native written documents were used in Mesoamerica, but no part of the continent north of central Mexico has been illuminated by those documents. For all that time and space we must rely upon the work of archaeologists or give up ever knowing how the cultural diversity of historic native Americans came about.

Because this is a volume in a bibliographic series on American Indian history, I have concentrated on prehistory. Students who find themselves attracted to topical areas of archaeology will find little to guide them here. Those who are developing interests in subjects such as ceramics, lithic technology, or early horticulture must seek specialized sources through the bibliographies of the more general works cited here.

The frequent confusion of North American archaeology with North American prehistory in the older literature resulted at least in part from an antiquarian bias. The purpose then was to find intrinsically interesting museum pieces. Interpretation of these pieces was not rigorous but was assigned to persons regarded as experts because they had seen other material of the same kind. It has been the nature of all disciplines of natural history that in the collecting phase of their development their leaders have had vast experience, encyclopedic memories, and often little commitment to rigorous logic and scientific method. But that time has long since passed, and modern archaeologists are not simply human data banks. American archaeology has been released from its confining identity with American prehistory to become a scientific process rather than a museum inventory. In consequence, archaeologists have turned more and more to examining things not related to American prehistory, in many cases things not previously thought of as the subject matter of archaeology at all. We now have historical archaeology, industrial archaeology, and even the above-ground archaeology of artifacts newly discarded in cities.

Archaeology and prehistory are therefore two very different things. Especially for materials introducing the student to archaeology, I have left out many works that are out-of-date or that draw too many examples from regions outside our continent. In doing this I have omitted a few that could be regarded as standard references for archaeology or even classics of their kind. But as archaeologists should know better than most others, time carries us all along, and the great works of a few years ago do not always serve the beginning student well.

I have avoided mentioning handbooks designed to instruct beginners in archaeological excavation techniques, particularly works implying that amateurs can and should attempt do-it-yourself fieldwork. Archaeology has reached the point in its development as a science where it is no longer possible for individuals to conduct productive and meaningful investigations without extensive training under professional supervision. Archaeological remains are a limited and irreplaceable resource that should not be subjected to destruction at the hands of untrained enthusiasts. Given the complexity of modern archaeology, the preservation and recovery of American prehistory simply cannot be left to amateurs.

I have also had to omit many sources that advanced students find essential to their work. This selectivity is required by the introductory nature of this bibliography, and the absence of many valuable sources does not mean I do not think them worthy. Sources omitted for these reasons include not only esoteric journal articles, but also many monographs that fill the shelves of libraries at major research universities and museums. For the most part these are concerned with archaeology rather than with prehistory and deal with highly complex and detailed problems rather than with synthesis. They form the bulk of publication by professional archaeologists, but turning to them without first reading introductory material would frustrate and confuse the beginning student. Most of the sources I have included are recently published, and their bibliographics will eventually lead serious students into the specialized literature.

My coverage of the field is necessarily spotty. I have insisted that all sources mentioned here be competently written, up-to-date, and nontechnical syntheses, and I am delighted that there are so many to choose from, given these strictures. Even so, many works that we wish existed still do not. I have not cited inferior works just to fill gaps, nor have I cited technical works in place of missing introductory snytheses, for neither of these measures would help the student new to the subject. It is unfortunate that many valuable local and regional syntheses have been published by little-known publishers and that the advertising and sale of their small runs has been geographically restricted. I have tracked down many of these, usually in the course of visiting sites, but it is likely that many more have escaped my notice. I regret these omissions but can do little about them. I only hope that those I have cited remain available in sufficient quantity to meet the demand this volume might produce.

Another large class of publications I have had to pass by includes the thin and inexpensive popular items put out by many museums. I own many such publications from (for example) the New York State Museum, the Milwaukee Public Museum, and the Arizona State Museum. These typically are written by professionals who seek to introduce the beginner to local prehistory, and they are suitable for high school libraries. But they are numerous, distributed only locally, and frequently revised. For all these reasons I have generally been unable to include specific citations here. Interested persons should ask the nearest archaeological museum for a listing of introductory booklets currently in print.

The bulletins and other publications of state and

local archaeological societies are often useful sources for those interested in prehistory on a regional scale. Most states and many cities have such organizations, but the quality of their publications varies greatly. I have too little space to mention them all here, and I would not like to recommend some over others even if I had space to do so. It is sufficient to say that archaeology has become a complex and difficult discipline in recent years, whereas the publications of archaeological societies have tended to retain an antiquarian outlook. High school and college librarians should consider obtaining publications from such organizations, however, because they are often a good source of information on local prehistory and a suitable introduction to regional prehistory. Librarians and others interested in collecting publications in this category should consult the nearest professional archaeologist(s), who will be able to recommend appropriate serial and single publications as well as to provide publishers' addresses. Folsom's guide to archaeological sites and museums [48] contains a list of official contacts. I hope this advice will help the reader avoid inappropriate publications while searching out appropriate but obscure publications that I either have missed or have not been able to include because of space limitations.

Most of the titles I have cited are books. Almost all the articles are available in volumes of collected readings. The reader is directed to these sources in two steps. The article cited appears in the bibliography with its original time and place of publication. An additional

line or two directs the reader to the volume(s) of collected readings where a reprint of the article can be
found. The beginning student should usually go first to
the reprints, because these are often edited extracts
from more difficult works. In some cases I have recommended volumes of collected readings without listing
separately all the articles they contain. In a few cases I
have cited only the volumes and their editors, since
separate citation of contents was unnecessary because of
the unity of their subject matter. Finally, a few comprehensive volumes contain chapters written by different authors specifically for those books. Although these
were not originally published as separate articles, I have
cited many of them separately and directed the reader
to them through the two steps described above. This
procedure ensures that important regional contributions will not be overlooked because they become lost
among others of the same type in large, comprehensive
works.

RECOMMENDED WORKS

For the Beginner

[21]   Claiborne, Robert, *The First Americans.*

[31]   Deetz, James, *Invitation to Archaeology.*

[48]   Folsom, Franklin, *America's Ancient Treasures.*

[158] Snow, Dean R., *The Archaeology of North America.*

[165] Stuart, George E., and Gene S. Stuart, *Discovering Man's Past in the Americas.*

For a Basic Library

[1]   Adams, Richard E. W., *Prehistoric Mesoamerica.*

[8]   Aveni, Anthony F., *Native American Astronomy.*

[11]   Brain, Jeffrey P., Peter Copeland, Louis de la Haba, Mary Ann Harrell, Tee Loftin, Jay Luvaas, and Douglas W. Schwartz, *Clues to America's Past.*

[42]   Fagan, Brian M., ed. *Corridors in Time.*

[46]   Fitting, James E., ed., *The Development of North American Archaeology.*

BIBLIOGRAPHICAL ESSAY

General Works on Archaeology

There is more to North American archaeology than most newcomers to the field think. To be sure, the prehistory of North America is interesting in its own right, and a large body of literature is devoted to its description. But archaeology is much more than the description of the debris of prehistory, and its richness depends upon much more than the existence of sites containing dazzling artifacts. If we sought only museum pieces, and if we aspired to the esthetic standards set by recent traveling exhibits from Egypt and China, North American archaeology would attract little international attention. As it happens, however, the large number of archaeological scholars and institutions in North America have put this continent in the lead worldwide. For archaeology as practiced in North America has long since been converted from a humanistic effort to a scientific one, and the interaction of so many scholars during this process has resulted in a body of literature that for size and complexity can scarcely be matched. Thus the relatively advanced development of North American archaeology has been less the result of the inherent qualities of the continent's prehistory than of commitment and interaction by many individuals and their supporting institutions.

Because, like so many other sciences, archaeology is well advanced in North America, a disproportionate amount of the relevant literature is written in English. This circumstance has given me much to choose from, something that is at once advantageous and difficult. I have had to eliminate many sources that could be considered superb examples of North American archaeology because although their theoretical bases, methods, techniques, and authors were all born here, they do not concentrate sufficiently on the prehistory of North America. There are books that would do much to illuminate the applications of the latest methods and techniques of North American archaeology but that draw too many of their examples from areas outside our continent. Similarly, many excellent articles that could illustrate the best efforts of North American archaeologists have had to be omitted because they treat some aspect of prehistory outside our area or draw too little upon examples from North America to be included here. In short, modern archaeologists have come more and more to define themselves in terms of the kinds of archaeological problems that interest them rather than in terms of regional or continental prehistory, and this international trend makes it more difficult to assemble regional bibliographies than it once was.

There are several relatively short basic introductions to modern scientific archaeology. *Invitation to Archaeology* [31], by James Deetz, has enjoyed enormous popularity since its publication in 1967. This book succeeds in taking the beginning student through and beyond discovery, excavation, and classification techniques and into the abstract concepts of space, time, form, context, function, and structure that underlie meaningful analysis. Although some of his ideas have never been generally accepted by other archaeologists, Deetz's presentation remains a good introduction for high school and beginning college students.

Two other basic introductions are Thomas's *Predicting the Past* [173] and Fagan's *Archaeology: A Brief Introduction* [44]. Both approach archaeology as anthropology, covering the basics of survey, excavation, dating, and preservation and then moving on to touch upon some of the more clearly scientific issues that concern modern professional archaeologists. For a more traditional introduction that stresses the reconstruction of prehistory over the issues of topical archaeology, refer to Irving Rouse's *Introduction to Prehistory: A Systematic Approach* [149]. Here the emphasis is on reconstructing extinct ethnic systems.

There are also several larger introductions to contemporary archaeology, all designed as introductory college textbooks. Frank Hole and Robert F. Heizer offer two such texts, *An Introduction to Prehistoric Archeology* [86], and *Prehistoric Archeology: A Brief Introduction* [87]. The first, now in its third edition, has been a popular introductory text since 1965. The second is a more recent attempt to provide a shorter introduction to fit situations where the older text was too large. In competition with both are Fagan's *In the Beginning* [41], now also in its third edition, Knudson's *Culture in Retrospect* [106], and Smith's *Foundations of Archaeology* [157]. All five introductions are appropriate for beginning college students, and choosing among them is largely a matter of personal preference and cost.

The rapid and sometimes dramatic changes in archaeology in recent years have made many archaeologists self-conscious and sometimes nostalgic about the discipline as it once was. The result has been a series of histories of American archaeology. These can be very useful to persons who are interested in the ways archaeology and society at large have influenced each other or who simply wish to evaluate older sources on North American prehistory. The dusty old tomes that deal with sunken continents and racially superior visitors to prehistoric America were as much a product of their times as the gaudy paperbacks pretending to demonstrate prehistoric visits from outer space are a product of ours. Willey and Sabloff's *A History of American Archaeology* [197] deals explicitly with the development of the discipline from 1492 to the date of publication (1974). Woodall's *An Introduction to Modern Archaeology* [201] does the same thing much more briefly and includes an equally brief example of explanation in contemporary archaeology. Woodall's book is not the comprehensive introduction to archaeology its title might suggest. Two volumes, *The Development of North American Archaeology* [46] and *Archaeological Researches in Retrospect* [196], contain separate articles by several authors dealing with the history of archaeological research in the various regions of North America. I mention each of these separately below under the appropriate regional headings. In *The Science of Archaeology?*

[124], Richard S. MacNeish gives us a highly personal account of his own growth and the development of his discipline that might interest students considering a career in archaeology. Finally, *The First Americans: A Story of North American Archaeology* [126], is a popular history of the development of American archaeology by Kurt W. Marek, the man who wrote *Gods, Graves, and Scholars.* The text is lucidly written, but the sections have been erratically assembled, and the beginner might be confused by the poor organization.

Archaeology has become a discipline over the objections of many. There are those in the profession today who would rather see it remain a kind of art history and who feel increasingly alienated as it becomes a science in its own right. Gone are the days when science in archaeology amounted to the part-time efforts of interested chemists, physicists, and the like. Gone too are the days when I frequently heard bookstore customers object that the archaeology books had been shelved with anthropology rather than with the art books, "where they belonged." In contrast to the retrospective histories of American archaeology, the past two decades have also produced books that attempt to summarize what is somewhat pompously known as the "new archaeology." Several books I have already cited attempt to do this in part, and several others that I will not cite have that as their only aim. Some of this is over the heads of beginners, while some of it is merely obscure. The beginner can avoid what some have called the "cumbersome litany" by reading David Wilson's *The New Archaeology*

[199]. Wilson is a science writer, not a professional archaeologist, and as such he is perhaps better able to judge and speak to his audience. Although the book does not fully address the complex theoretical issues that are at the heart of current controversy, it does convey much of the excitement that has been generated by new scientific techniques and the breakthroughs they have produced. Students ready to begin reading the articles professionals write for each other can start with volumes of collected readings. Two good choices are Fagan's *Corridors in Time* [42] and Green's *In Search of Man* [65].

The recent revolution in archaeology is often said to have begun with Walter Taylor's *A Study of Archeology* [171], originally published as a memoir of the American Anthropological Association. Taylor's study made many archaeologists uneasy. There was a feeling that something had to be done to get archaeology out of its rut of collecting and classifying, but few had any clear idea of how this was to be accomplished. We discovered that changing the spelling to "archeology" was merely cosmetic. The *American Anthropologist* went back to the old spelling in 1973, by which time the revolution was well under way and "archeology" began to look like the last pretense of a worn-out approach to the discipline.

Students who are even more advanced might wish to test their critical skills and at the same time learn something more of the history of American archaeology. The discipline has many roots in the nineteenth century, but it is now clear that much of what was written then was nonsense. Some of it is occasionally revived in support of religious preconceptions, extraterrestrial fantasies, and other nonscientific purposes. Many of the scattered sources that make up the naive youth of American archaeology have been assembled into two loose-leaf volumes by William R. Corliss titled *Strange Artifacts* [27]. Some intellectual sophistication is required if these sources are to be used properly, and Corliss does little to counterbalance their breathless enthusiasm. It is unlikely that high school students are capable of seeing through the frauds, misinterpretations, and absurdities that litter these articles. Nevertheless, they remain useful to sober investigators trying to get at the origins of the myths of prehistory—past and present.

A more appropriate book for the beginner is Wauchope's amusing *Lost Tribes and Sunken Continents* [185], a compilation of many of the frauds and follies of nineteenth-century archaeology in America. Silverberg's *Mound Builders of Ancient America* [155] deals with the history of just one set of these topics, in which the burial and temple mounds of the Eastern Woodlands were attributed to a lost race of builders. The presumption at the time was that American Indians were inferior savages and therefore could not have been responsible for the impressive sites of the East. McKusick's *The Davenport Conspiracy* [119] is an interesting account of how racism, greed, and gullibility combined in one instance to destroy reputations and damage rational archaeology. All three books are recommended reading for anyone tempted by currently popular books that pretend to prove that American Indians were hosts to foreign visitors before 1492.

It is sometimes forgotten that native Americans did not cease to exist with the end of prehistory and that the current interest in historical archaeology has some relevance to them. Historical archaeology was not always as respectable as it is today, partly because America has less historical time depth than some other parts of the world. Fortunately, many archaeologists are now as interested in historic native Americans as they are in transplanted Europeans. *Historical Archaeology* [91] and *A Guide to Artifacts of Colonial America* [92], both by Ivor Noël Hume, are good starting points for those interested in historical archaeology. References to the archaeology of specific historical native American cultures can be found in appropriate later sections of this essay.

The major themes of American archaeology (as opposed to American prehistory) have been made available to the high school beginner in the National Geographic Society's *Clues to America's Past* [11]. The examples are all drawn from American prehistory and history, but the primary emphasis is on how the archaeologist does his job, not on cultural sequences.

Archaeology is in a golden age of sorts. The stimulating if sometimes clumsy pioneer works of the new archaeology are behind us, and publishers' lists of books in print offer an array of interesting new approaches. In place of the old culture histories and art histories with their vague and often untested interpretive statements, we now have scientifically rigorous syntheses and topical works by the dozen. It is still possible for one mind to comprehend it all, and so it is an exciting time for professional archaeologists whose feet have not taken root in the assumptions of the old archaeology. Still, it will not be long before the discipline has expanded to a point where no one person can cover it all, and it will necessarily begin to break up into specialized subdisciplines. We have clues, but we still cannot predict with any certainty what those subdisciplines will be.

General Works on North American Prehistory

People have been in the New World for fewer than 30,000 years, a very brief period compared with the long evolution of humanity in the Old World. The reason is that bands of hunters could not expand northeastward across the Bering Strait region until mankind generally had reached the biological and cultural levels necessary for life in the Arctic. Thus the first Americans were relatively sophisticated hunters who shared a long prehistory with those people remaining behind in the Old World. Chard's *Man in Prehistory* [20] summarizes the long development of humanity in the Old World for those looking for the background development of the first Americans. Hester's *Introduction to Archaeology* [82], in fact mostly an introduction to prehistory, does much the same thing. However, Hester's book tends to be more detailed, which might confuse the beginner. Both books are a few years out of date despite their recent copyright dates, and both contain chapters on the Old World that do not bear directly on New World prehistory.

General works on North American prehistory vary greatly in scope and approach. *Discovering Man's Past in the Americas* [165] is a well-illustrated short summary of New World prehistory for the beginner at the high school level. Sanders and Marino's *New World Prehistory* [151] is also short, but it is essentially unillustrated and is designed for more sophisticated readers. Both attempt to generalize on the whole of New World prehistory, but whereas the first book is a relatively simple synthesis, the second is organized around particular theoretical considerations that make it both more profound and more controversial. Between these two is Meggers's *Prehistoric America* [129], a brief summary of New World prehistory that emphasizes the civilizations of Mexico and Peru but also has a compact and easily read summary for North America. Unlike Sanders and Marino, Meggers tends to leave current controversies unresolved rather than stating her own interpretations. An exception is her acceptance of a diffusionist perspective generally and transpacific contacts in particular, something about which many archaeologists remain doubtful.

Attempts to cover all of New World prehistory in more detail usually appear as edited volumes containing contributions from several authors. Although both are in print, Jennings's *Ancient Native Americans* [98] is designed to replace the older *Prehistoric Man in the New World* [100] edited by Jennings and Norbeck. Both volumes emphasize North America but have chapters on Mesoamerica and South America as well. They share roughly the same regional chapter headings, but the more recent book mostly contains contributions from younger authors, and a comparison of regional chapters indicates the kinds of progress made in archaeology over the course of fourteen years. Individual chapters from *Ancient Native Americans* are cited below with other regional works.

North America [61], edited by Gorenstein, is a briefer compilation of articles by different authors. In this case the continent is divided into only four large regions, and Mexico does not receive separate treatment. The level of synthesis is appropriate for beginners.

New World Archaeology: Theoretical and Cultural Transformations [204] is a collection of articles originally published separately in issues of *Scientific American*. All are comprehensible to the beginner. Although there is no pretense of general or uniform coverage, the articles highlight specific regional prehistories. The more recent ones reveal the shifts in scientific archaeology that I discussed earlier. Some of them are mentioned individually below.

Few writers attempt to synthesize all of New World prehistory in one single-author work. Gordon Willey has done so in his two-volume *An Introduction to American Archaeology*. Only volume 1, *North and Middle America* [195], is directly relevant here. Willey has carried out his own research in both North America and Mesoamerica and appreciates more than most the profound influence

Mexico had on developments in North America over the past 3,000 years. There is a separate chapter on Mesoamerica. Willey's approach tends to be detailed, technological, and cultural-historical compared with more recent trends toward the synthesis of processes and away from sequences of material remains. College-level readers can choose between reading the book from cover to cover and selecting regional chapters without having to adjust for the different styles and perspectives of several authors. The book is well-illustrated with photos and drawings.

My own *Archaeology of North America* [158] attempts to summarize for the beginner both traditional prehistory and some of the more recent analyses of process. Mexican influences are noted and explained, but there is no separate section discussing Mesoamerica. Illustrations were chosen more for their beauty than for their scientific significance. Jennings's *Prehistory of North America* [97] stands between my summary and that of Gordon Willey. It shares many illustrations with *Ancient Native Americans* [98], but none of them are photographs. Like Willey, Jennings is more concerned with cultural sequences than with process, and the result is a fairly comprehensive summary of the framework of prehistory north of Mexico. Finally, Claiborne's *The First Americans* [21] is for the beginner reading at a high school level. The book is one of the Emergence of Man series published by Time-Life, and it suffers from dramatic overstatement in some places and misleading simplification in others. It is nonetheless an appropriate starting point for young readers.

Some general works on North American ethnology begin with discussions of prehistory. Readers who wish to approach prehistory as background for stronger interests in ethnology may find these more appropriate than the prehistories I have mentioned so far. Garbarino's *Native American Heritage* [56] presents just such a summary of prehistory as a prologue to a synthesis of North American ethnology. The book is in the established tradition of American ethnography and is suitable for high school students. Jennings provides the same kind of prehistoric introduction to ethnology in Spencer and Jennings's *The Native Americans* [160]. This volume, now in its second edition, is more difficult and therefore is suitable for college-level beginners.

Folsom's guide to archaeological sites and museums [48] is appropriate for readers at and above the high school level. It is organized into seven regional chapters covering Canada and the United States. Emphasis is upon sites and museums regularly open to the public, with directions to each and short articles explaining their significance. The text is liberally and informatively illustrated and has forty-three "features," each a brief essay on a specific aspect of prehistory. Thus there is one on Anasazi religion, another on radiocarbon dating, and still another on Adena culture. The book contains a bibliography and a list of official contacts in archaeology for each state in the United States. For some reason Canada has been left out here.

There are many books written from an art history perspective that touch upon prehistoric artifacts from North America. But most books dealing with North

American Indian art concentrate upon artifacts from the historic period. Most of those dealing specifically with prehistoric artifacts concentrate on items from Mesoamerica and highland South America. Thus there are few I can recommend as sources fully relevant to North American prehistory. William Teel has compiled a series of useful photographs for the University Prints and has written a commentary to accompany them [172]. Photos of sites and artifacts from North America are included in the University Prints, series N, section 3. These photos can be ordered individually on twenty-seven leaves as a supplement to written works. Ralph T. Coe's *Sacred Circles* [24] is a catalog of artifacts gathered for a showing in London and Kansas City. Most of the photographs are of historic artifacts, but a large minority show prehistoric items. All artifacts are unusually well photographed and described, and their regional grouping gives the reader a good feel for the continuities in material culture from prehistory into history. Miles's *Indian and Eskimo Artifacts of North America* [131] provides extensive photographic coverage and enough text to explain it. It is a good cross section of both prehistoric and historic artifact classes.

The rock art of North American Indians lies somewhere between art and archaeology. The literature on this subject is widely scattered, and anyone seriously interested in it will have to master library search techniques. Grant's *Rock Art of the American Indian* [64] is a good starting point. It covers both painted "pictographs" and engraved "petroglyphs" from the scattered and predominantly naturalistic examples of the Eastern Woodlands to the usually more abstract forms of the West.

Libraries and serious students should watch for the publication of volumes of the forthcoming *Handbook of North American Indians*. This Smithsonian Institution series will eventually run to about twenty volumes, issued as each is ready rather than in serial order. The California volume [78] is first, followed by the Northeast [175] volume and other regional treatments in no particular order. Each will contain separate chapters on specific tribes as well as chapters on prehistory that show how historic tribes relate to prehistoric developments. The books are very reasonably priced by today's standards, and the set should be a standard reference for any basic library collection concerned with North American prehistory and the historic cultures it led up to.

Regardless of their low prices and titillating subjects, the current spate of paperback books that pretend to be on the frontiers of archaeological discovery should be avoided. Those claiming extraterrestrial origins for certain aspects of prehistory are particularly pernicious concoctions of fantasy, contrived data selection, and deliberate fraud. Those that promote hypothetical transoceanic voyages before Columbus are not often the products of serious scholarship, and they tend to be inspired by the promise of royalty checks. For North America the most recent surge in this kind of writing has concentrated upon ninetcenth- and twentieth-century stone structures in New England and the pre-Columbian Celtic voyages they are supposed to suggest. In fact, the only possibly convincing evidence of pre-Columbian voyages to North America relates to the supposed Norse remains from northern Newfoundland. Ingstad's *The Discovery of a Norse Settlement in America* [93] is a scholarly treatment of these finds. But even the presumed Norse finds remain unconvincing to some archaeologists. Magnusson's *Viking Expansion Westwards* [125] is a very cautious examination of that evidence, and although it is suitable for high school readers it is a scholarly work that can be appreciated by more advanced students as well. Casson's "The Lure of the Vikings" [17], "Who Got Here First?" [16], and "Who First Crossed the Oceans?" [18] are all popular articles that treat the subject in a readable and well-illustrated yet sober way. Certainly the flamboyant exploits of Thor Heyerdahl and similar sources should be treated skeptically and never acquired in lieu of trustworthy sources on prehistory. Three sources on the subject of transoceanic contacts before Columbus that I do regard as trustworthy are Jett's "Pre-Columbian Transoceanic Contacts" [101], Ekholm's "Transpacific Contacts" [40], and Meggers and Evans's "A Transpacific Contact in 3000 B.C." [130]. I do not necessarily agree with the views expressed by any of them, but these at least are sober professionals, not cheap sensationalists.

Pseudolinguistics is another trap for the beginning reader. I have seen a seven-volume work pretending to show that the languages of the Algonkian family derive from the Germanic languages of Scandinavia, and also papers by a man who insists this is silly and goes on to claim they derive from Portuguese. There are many such works, and their authors come from the same cloth as those who imagine they see Norse runes on boulders where the rest of us see only plow scratches. A much better introduction to the historical linguistics of North America is Swadesh's "Linguistic Overview" [166]. Several of the basic introductory works cited here also deal rationally with historical linguistics.

Students interested in archaeoastronomy in North America, a subject often exploited by pseudoscientists, would do well to consult Aveni's *Native American Astronomy* [8]. Aveni has also compiled and edited *Archaeoastronomy in Pre-Columbian America* [7]. E. C. Krupp's *In Search of Ancient Astronomies* [110] is a clear and successful attempt to undercut currently popular pseudoscientific nonsense by presenting a sober and honest summary of archaeoastronomy under a popular title. The book demonstrates that writers can both entertain and educate their readers without making fools of them.

Mesoamerican Background

The prehistory of North America cannot be understood without the backdrop of Mesoamerica in general and Mexico in particular. All native Americans began with a shared hunting-and-gathering base more than

20,000 years ago, but because of advantages of climate and wild plants some areas advanced toward agriculture and settled life more rapidly than others. Plant domesticates, most notably corn (maize), beans, and squash, were developed first in Mexico and only later spread northward into temperate North America. With them spread architectural, artistic, and other influences. Thus the prehistoric people of North America cannot be fully understood in isolation from the earlier Mexican developments that influenced them so profoundly.

Most introductory books on North American prehistory include chapters on Mesoamerica. The chapters by Culbert [29] and Armillas [4] in edited compilations are useful brief introductions. Weaver and Adams both provide us with single-author introductory volumes on Mesoamerica [186], [1]. Both are up-to-date and well illustrated, but most readers using them as background for North America should read them selectively, steering away from the Mayan material. Readers who stay with the Mexican portions of these introductions are certain to perceive the important links to the Eastern Woodlands, the Southwest, and beyond.

The emergence of food production in Mexico was a particularly important development. We owe much to Richard MacNeish for his extensive work on this topic. His popular articles in *Scientific American* [120] and *Archaeology* [122] are excellent summaries of his discoveries for the beginner. Coe's popular article on the Olmecs [23] is a good introduction to the culture that dominated Mexico during the first of three great periods of Mexican civilization, the Formative Period. Two similar treatments by Pfeiffer [138] and Millon [132] can be used to introduce the beginner to the following Classic Period, during which the great city of Teotihuacán dominated central Mexico and influenced developments far to the north. The Post-Classic Period, dominated at its end by the Aztec empire, was terminated by the Spanish conquest. Coe's "The Chinampas of Mexico" [22] describes the agricultural underpinnings of that last great native empire and shows the beginner by comparison with MacNeish's articles how far food production had come since its beginnings in the Tehuacán Valley.

The Earliest Americans

Most of the general works on North American prehistory begin with chapters on first arrivals and the Paleo-Indian period. Some old sources on the subject are still in print, but those predating 1970 should be avoided. Many of the sites mentioned in earlier sources have since been discredited. More recently discovered sites do not appear at all in the older sources, and interpretations generally tend to be out-of-date. Thus, although there are old sources that deal exclusively with the earliest Americans, they should be avoided in favor of relevant chapters in more recent works. Forbis's "The Paleoamericans" [50] and Jennings's "Origins" [99] are both brief introductions for the beginner.

MacNeish's *Early Man in America* [123] pulls together ten articles on the subject that were originally published in *Scientific American*. Some are much more recent than others, and partly for this reason there are several important contradictions in the collection. Readers should avoid the three articles from the 1950s, which contain conclusions that have been disproved by more recent work. Even without these three old articles, however, the remaining seven show the range of interpretations favored by different scholars in recent years. For example, while Haynes [75] sees little evidence for a human population in the New World before 12,000 years ago, MacNeish [121] concludes that early Americans might have pushed through North America and into South America by as early as 22,000 years ago. It should be noted that all but two of the articles in this volume are also available in the larger collection of *Scientific American* articles entitled *New World Archaeology: Theoretical and Cultural Transformations* [204]. An article by Wheat [193] on the Olsen-Chubbuck site appears in both, and the monograph [194] from which this article was derived has been abstracted for inclusion in both of the collections mentioned earlier. Ogburn's "The First Discovery of America" is an article on paleo-Indians suitable for beginners [135]. It is reprinted in one of the collections, but without the illustrations that accompanied the original article. Haag's *Scientific American* article [69] on the Bering Strait land bridge remains an excellent introduction for the younger reader even though his 1962 prediction of the eventual discovery of

50,000-year-old human remains in America now seems excessive. I doubt that mankind has been in America for more than 27,000 years.

Although I disagree with some of its conclusions, Tolstoy's "From the Old World to the New World via Bering Strait" [174] is a useful essay on the circumpolar diffusion of certain culture traits. Although published in 1975, the article appears to have been written well before then. Most archaeologists have long since discarded the possibility that the ceramics of the Northeast were derived either from Siberia or from across the Atlantic.

Wilmsen's thin volume on the Lindenmeier site [198] appears to be an introduction to this important paleo-Indian campsite for beginning students. Unfortunately, it is likely to be confusing to the beginner. It is the only readily available monograph on the site, but it should be read only after most of the other sources mentioned here.

The Casper Site [53] by George C. Frison is an excellent site report that can serve as a model in several ways. The site is a 10,000-year-old late paleo-Indian bison kill that was discovered by amateur archaeologists. What followed that discovery was a rare example of productive cooperation between amateurs and professionals. The resulting book is also a prime example of a paleo-Indian site report, the use of faunal remains by archaeologists, and the application of modern archaeological method. Paleo-Indian hunters carrying unfluted Hell Gap points used the parabolic sand dune at the site as a natural trap. Repeated use of the site for bison drives eventually led to the killing and butchering of at least seventy-four individuals of the now-extinct *Bison bison antiquus*. Students will find few examples to follow that are as good as this one.

Regional Works

Regional prehistories are often defined in terms of state boundaries. This reflects the political realities of funding but is unfortunate in that it tends to divide certain natural geographic regions while lumping others. Thus there may be no single source that covers the prehistory of a particular stretch of the Mississippi, because the river is used as a state boundary. Conversely, New York's prehistory has been treated in a single volume even though there are many contrasts between the prehistory of Long Island and that of the Niagara frontier.

There is terminological inconsistency among even general introductory works, and that inconsistency is even greater when regional works are compared. Words like "stage," "period," and "tradition" are often used with only implicit definitions, and even when definitions are explicit one cannot count on consistency. It is the reader's task to assume little and to resolve confusion whenever possible by working back to more general sources.

The Eastern Woodlands

Basic introductions to the prehistory of the Eastern Woodlands such as that by Forbis [49] can be found in the general works on North American prehistory mentioned above. Griffin's summary article in *Science* [67] remains an excellent introduction for the beginner. Unfortunately it is not available in a book of collected readings. However his chapters in *Ancient Native Americans* [68] and *Prehistoric Man in the New World* [66], which concentrate on the northern part of the Eastern Woodlands, serve almost as well. These volumes also offer separate basic introductions to the prehistory of the Southeast by Jon D. Muller [133] and by William H. Sears [154]. David S. Brose [13] and James B. Stoltman [162] provide histories of archaeological research in the northern and the southern parts of the Eastern Woodlands. Both provide a useful perspective on changing concepts and approaches over the past century and a half of archaeological research in the East.

Although the title suggests much broader coverage, Brennan's *Artifacts of Prehistoric America* [12] is essentially a picturebook of artifacts from the Northeast woodlands. To be sure, there are artifacts from other parts of North America, but readers expecting uniform coverage will be disappointed. There are many large and well explained, if somewhat muddy, illustrations, and chapter 3 contains one of the few clear expositions of the use of the spear thrower I have encountered.

Having read the basic introductions, most readers will want to turn to volumes that treat smaller regions within the Eastern Woodlands. Coverage here is not uniform. Volume 15 of the *Handbook of North American Indians* [175] contains summaries of the prehistory of the Northeast, and, when finished, a new series being edited by James B. Griffin should provide relatively uniform coverage of the larger region. For the present, the key work on the Northeast is William A. Ritchie's *The Archaeology of New York State* [144]. The 1969 edition is slightly more up-to-date than the original 1965 edition, although the latter has a much better index. Both are out of print and available only in libraries and in bookstores specializing in used books. Unfortunately, Ritchie's prose is always densely laden with technical jargon. He makes no concessions to a nonspecialist reader. Ritchie's *The Archaeology of Martha's Vineyard* [145] provides a view of New England prehistory that is parochial but nevertheless illustrates the archaeology of coastal New England sites. Ritchie and Funk's *Aboriginal Settlement Patterns in the Northeast* [146] is more technical but is still in print. Tuck's "The Iroquois Confederacy" [177] provides a simplified discussion of an archaeological approach to the formation of an important prehistoric political organization. From there the student might wish to move on to the same author's *Onondaga Iroquois Prehistory* [178], a serious attempt to tie the late prehistory of central New York to Iroquois ethnohistory. A similar attempt to link the archaeology and history of southern New England can be found in

Simmon's *Cautantowwit's House* [156]. This book concentrates on the excavation and analysis of an early historic Indian burial ground on an island in Narragansett Bay, Rhode Island. Still another such attempt is *Cartier's Hochelaga and the Dawson Site* [136], an explicit attempt to determine whether the site on the Saint Lawrence was the one the explorer visited in 1535. Salwen's "Sea Levels and Archaeology in the Long Island Sound Area" [150] gives the advanced reader an introduction to the literature on Northeast coastal ecology.

Foundations of Pennsylvania Prehistory [104] is an edited compilation of articles on the subject. The volume was published in 1971, but many of its chapters are much older. Fortunately, the editors had the sense and skill to standardize and update chapters without destroying their originality. Turnbaugh's 1975 monograph [180] is an in-depth analysis of the prehistory of one part of north-central Pennsylvania.

The mid-Atlantic states are treated in an introductory way by only a few sources. Lewis's *A Handbook for Delmarva Archaeology* [113] is appropriate for the beginner. Students are also apt to encounter the recent (1968) republication of Weslager's *Delaware's Buried Past* [192]. Beginners should not be directed to this book, but more advanced students might read it in order to appreciate how far archaeology has come in recent decades. A far better source for the beginner is Kraft's *A Delaware Indian Symposium* [107], which begins with a summary of New Jersey prehistory and leads the reader into ethnohistory.

Fitting's *The Archaeology of Michigan* [45] synthesizes the prehistory of that state from the point of view of a single archaeologist but succeeds in conveying the range of approaches taken by various archaeologists. The book is useful for relatively advanced readers seeking an introduction to the prehistory of the upper Great Lakes region. In contrast to this volume, Johnson's *The Prehistoric Peoples of Minnesota* [102] and Ritzenthaler's *Prehistoric Indians of Wisconsin* [147] are both very brief introductions to state prehistories that are designed for readers at the high school level. Between these extremes is Quimby's *Indian Life in the Upper Great Lakes* [141], a general and very readable introduction to the prehistory of the region. Quimby also gives us *Indian Culture and European Trade Goods* [142], which covers both archaeology and ethnology in the upper Great Lakes from about A.D. 1600 to 1820.

Stuart Struever's large-scale excavations at and around the Koster site in southwestern Illinois have attracted considerable popular attention in recent years. For the professional audience, Struever and his team have produced serious scientific papers such as "Woodland Subsistence-Settlement Systems in the Lower Illinois Valley" [163]. Through popular articles, television appearances and the recent publication of a monograph on the Koster site [164], Struever and his colleague, Felicia Antonelli Holton, have filled a large gap in the general public's awareness of the importance of archaeological excavation in the Midwest. Advanced students should also consult Houart's 1971 technical report on the site [89] as well as scientific papers emerging from the project such as those by David A. Asch [5] and Jane E. Buikstra [14].

The heartland of the Eastern Woodland is the Ohio River drainage. It is the setting for the Indian Knoll site, an archaic period site dating roughly 2000– 3500 B.C. that is famous for having stimulated archaeological thinking on prehistoric ecological adaptation. Webb's classic 1946 site report is once again available in a 1974 edition [187]. The Ohio drainage is also the setting for the later Adena and Hopewell cultures. Both featured monumental earthworks and exotic grave goods, and both had wide-ranging influence on contemporaneous cultures via extensive trade networks. *Ohio's Prehistoric Peoples* [139] summarizes these and other prehistoric developments in Ohio for the high school reader. More detailed but somewhat outdated summaries of Adena culture are to be found in *The Adena People* [189], *The Adena People No. 2.* [188], and *Mounds for the Dead* [34]. *Adena: The Seeking of an Identity* [167], although not without its own errors, is a more technical and more up-to-date summary. Haag's "The Adena Culture" [70] is a retrospective summary of archaeological research on Adena sites that is sophisticated without being highly technical.

Indiana's Prehistoric Past [168] is another thin volume supposedly written at a high school level. So many specialized terms are crammed into the little book, however, that one needs a substantial background to understand it. This has prompted one reviewer to remark that if you can understand this book you need not read it.

Adena and Hopewell are known for their use of native copper and other metals. The use of copper depended upon its natural occurrence in northern Michigan and elsewhere, and it was first used by the earlier Old Copper culture of that area. Easby's article on New World metallurgy [38] discusses this development and related technology in Mesoamerica and in Central and South America.

Both Adena and Hopewell are discussed in Fagan's popularized "Who Were the Mound Builders?" [43]. Hopewell sites have for some reason not inspired the same number of books as Adena sites except for highly technical volumes. Prufer's "The Hopewell Cult" [140] is perhaps the best brief introduction to the subject. Other summaries can be found in the more general works cited earlier.

Part of the Adena-Hopewell area is covered in Swauger's *Rock Art of the Upper Ohio Valley* [169]. This is a detailed regional treatment of petroglyphs and pictographs that provides serious students with a basis of comparison with rock art in other parts of North America. A narrower but more informative source is the Vastokas's *Sacred Art of the Algonkians* [181]. This analysis of a single site from Ontario goes further toward explaining petroglyph motifs, particularly those with heavy sexual content, than do most sources. My own "Rock Art and the Power of Shamans" [159] is a similar attempt to go beyond a simple inventory of motifs.

The northern fringe of the Eastern Woodlands lies in southern Canada. Some of the sources already mentioned treat parts of this area. In addition to these, beginners should look to Wright's *Ontario Prehistory* [203], which presents a lucid and simplified overview of that province. There are unfortunately no comparable volumes for Quebec and the Maritime Provinces. Tuck's "An Archaic Indian Cemetery in Newfoundland" [176] discusses an extraordinary archaic period burial site that is related to similar sites in the Maritimes and New England. "An Archaic Indian Burial Mound in Labrador" [179] discusses an even older (5000 B.C.) site that pushes the origins of mound construction much farther back than had previously been suspected. It may well be that this early development on the fringes of the subarctic eventually inspired Adena mound-building, a heritage that would make hypotheses regarding Mexican or other sources of inspiration largely unnecessary. Unfortunately the second of these two articles is not yet available in a volume of collected reprints. For the woodlands west of Ontario, students have the volume of collected papers entitled *Ten Thousand Years: Archaeology in Manitoba* [85].

The southern part of the Eastern Woodlands, the Southeast, is often treated as a separate region of North America. Sears's [154], Willey's [195], and Muller's [133] chapters on the subject do so quite clearly, as already mentioned. The distinctiveness of the Southeast is largely the result of the last thousand years of prehistory when Mexican influences led to the emergence of large agricultural communities and the construction of huge temple mounds. The portable artifacts of the later periods also show exotic Mexican influences. The common features of late prehistoric cultures in the Southeast have been described and illustrated in *Sun Circles and Human Hands* [55]. Hudson's *The Southeastern Indians* [90] provides a substantial prehistoric background to the ethnological summaries that are the main components of the book. What was perhaps the largest of the Southeast communities is in fact outside the Southeast as defined by some of these authors. Cahokia, as the site is now called, has been briefly described in Pfeiffer's "America's First City" [137] and Fowler's "A Pre-Columbian Urban Center on the Mississippi" [51], both of which are accessible to most readers. Single volumes on Cahokia and other major Southeast sites such as Etowah, Georgia, and Moundville, Alabama, are now in preparation. Walthall's popular monograph on Moundville [182] will serve the beginner until something more substantial is in print. At the same time, Larson's analysis of social stratification at Etowah [111] serves to introduce that site and indicate the kinds of problems archaeologists are now probing at large ceremonial centers.

Considerable attention has been given to the Cherokee and their prehistoric ancestors. The Cherokee are linguistic relatives of the Iroquois despite their historic participation in the broader cultural developments of the Southeast. Keel's *Cherokee Archaeology* [103] and Dickens's *Cherokee Prehistory* [33] are technical and relatively difficult works on the subject. These and similar efforts are a refreshing alternative to syntheses that are defined by modern state boundaries.

Many readers will be attracted by the highly visual *The Material Culture of Key Marco Florida* [59]. This is a unique site in which the high water table has preserved extraordinary artifacts of wood, shell, bone, antler, and other materials that ordinarily perish very quickly. Many of the articles recovered are otherwise unknown in the Southeast.

The Great Plains

Frison's chapter "The Plains" [52] in *The Development of North American Archaeology* is a good introduction to the history of archaeological research in the region. His book *Prehistoric Hunters of the High Plains* [54] is the first in a projected series entitled New World Archaeological Record, and like the other volumes planned for the series it provides a basic introduction to the prehistory of one region of North America. The book concentrates on the northwestern Great Plains and is organized topically more than by time periods; it is an excellent in-depth introduction for the serious student. Waldo R. Wedel's introductory chapters on the Plains [190, 191] are more traditional chronological treatments of the prehistory of the region and therefore more suitable for the beginner.

There are several other regional syntheses for subdivisions of the Great Plains. One of these is Lehmer's

Introduction to Middle Missouri Archeology [112], a synthesis of work carried out ahead of dam construction in the Dakotas. Most of the sites excavated and described here have been erased by rising artificial lakes. Thus the late prehistoric and historic villages of the Mandans, Hidatsas, and Arikaras are in many instances now removed from the archaeological record. Lehmer's book must be read carefully, but the serious student will find it a useful introduction to regional prehistory, an interesting chapter in the history of American archaeological research, and more than a little poignant.

Prehistoric Villages in Eastern Nebraska [62] is a similar volume that deals with the prehistoric and historic villages of tribes such as the Pawnees and Poncas. Here too the emphasis is on the archaeology of the agricultural villages of the large river valleys of the eastern Plains. One interesting aspect of late prehistory in this area is the connection, both linguistic and archaeological, between the Pawnees and the Arikaras to the north of them. *The Dynamics of Stylistic Change in Arikara Ceramics* [30] by Deetz is an attempt to demonstrate the common origins of the two groups and plot their separate developments as independent tribes through ceramic analysis. The attempt does not succeed in all respects, but this brief analytical monograph does much to bridge the space between the descriptive treatments of eastern Nebraska and the middle Missouri while at the same time illustrating the kinds of problems that interest contemporary archaeologists.

There are also some works dealing with Plains

prehistory in terms of modern states. Chapman's *The Archaeology of Missouri*, volume 1 [19], is a basic introductory volume for the state that takes us to 1000 b.c. Unfortunately we do not yet have the promised second volume treating the next 3,000 years of Missouri prehistory. Wood's *Prehistoric Man and His Environments* [200] deals with the whole prehistoric sequence, but it is more technical and treats only the western Ozark highlands of central Missouri.

Men of Ancient Iowa [118] is a synthesis of the prehistory of that state. Although the eastern part of Iowa is properly part of the Eastern Woodlands, much of the state is on the Plains. Indeed, the state illustrates one of the difficulties we have when defining prehistoric regions. Some authors treat all or part of the Plains as an extension of the Eastern Woodlands because the village tribes that lived there in late prehistory were in many ways derived from the Woodlands and because the historic horsemen of the Plains were in many cases also displaced easterners. The mounted Plains Indian, regarded as the quintessential native American by filmmakers, was largely a phenomenon of the historic period. Haines summarizes what we know of the shallow prehistory and ethnohistory of these tribes in *The Plains Indians* [71].

The Desert West

This great dry province of North America lies between the Rocky Mountains and the coastal ranges of the Pacific states. It includes the Great Basin, where for the most part cultures remained at a hunting-and-gathering level of subsistence into the historic period. However, it also includes the Southwest, where agriculture and settled life were the rule for as much as 2,000 years. The prehistory of the region is summarized by Jennings in his chapter "The Desert West" [96], and an extract from his landmark *Danger Cave* [95] monograph is available in one of the volumes of collected readings I have included here. Authors such as Irwin [94] and Aikens [2] include that part of the Desert West that lies outside the Southwest in their separate chapters, each of which is entitled "The Far West." This reflects a recent tendency to lump the prehistories of both the Great Basin and the Northwest Plateau with that of coastal California, Oregon, and Washington. Most introductory books treat the Southwest as a separate region regardless of how they might handle the rest of the Desert West. Thus we have chapters on the Southwest by Lipe [114], Reed [143], and Washburn [184] in three introductory volumes.

The history of research in the Desert West generally and the Southwest in particular is important for a complete understanding of the many works on prehistory that have come out of the region over the years. Fortunately we have Rohn's history of archaeology "The Southwest and Intermontane West" [148] and Martin's more specific "Early Development in Mogollon Research" [127]. The latter sketches the history of research for one of the three primary prehistoric traditions of the

Southwest. Both help the beginner understand the changing goals of archaeological research in this region through the middle decades of the twentieth century.

Tree-ring dating is used more in the Southwest than in any other region of North America. Students wishing to understand this specialized dating technique and its implications should consult Bannister's article [10]. Those looking for a more visual introduction to the details of Southwest prehistory have the popular account of "Chaco Canyon's Mysterious Highways" [39].

Ancient Indians of the Southwest [170] is a brief introduction for the young reader but is so well written and illustrated that it can be enjoyed by anyone. From this the beginner can graduate to one of the several more ambitious syntheses of Southwestern prehistory. One can trace both the accumulation of new archaeological evidence and the rapid changes in archaeological aims from Gladwin's 1957 *A History of the Ancient Southwest* [60] through later volumes by Wormington [202] and McGregor [117] to Martin and Plog's 1973 version of archaeology in the Southwest [128]. Students interested in pottery types, chronologies, and geographic distributions should stay with the earlier summaries. Those more interested in problems of cultural process should consult the most recent. Perhaps more than any other region of North America, the Southwest shows us that the writing of prehistory no longer involves only the simple accumulation of archaeological facts and figures. The abundance of archaeological data in the Southwest has made it an important laboratory for testing complex new hypotheses, and future books will almost certainly continue the trends we can observe in Martin and Plog's volume. Students wishing to follow those trends a bit further have Longacre's work at the Carter Ranch site [115] and his analysis of an Apache wickiup [116]. There is also Hill's work at Broken K Pueblo [84] and Haury's older but still valuable analysis of the evidence for prehistoric migration at Point of Pines [73].

Some regard the Southwest as more an extension of Mesoamerica than a part of North America. The relationship with Mexico is clear in all the introductory chapters and books cited thus far. In most instances it is clear that of the three major Southwestern traditions, the Hohokam was the most strongly influenced by Mesoamerica, the Anasazi and Mogollon being somewhat further removed. The single most important Hohokam site is Snaketown, near Phoenix, and an excellent summary of Emil W. Haury's excavations at Snaketown is now available in a single volume [74].

As in most regions of North America, the rock art of the Desert West has been largely published apart from archaeological works. Schaafsma's *The Rock Art of Utah* [152] is drawn from the fieldwork of Donald Scott, which covered Utah and parts of Colorado, Nevada, and Arizona. *Rock Art in New Mexico* [153] by the same author observes state boundaries a bit more carefully. The first volume has both drawings and photographs, whereas the second is illustrated mainly with photographs. *Prehistoric Rock Art of Nevada and Eastern California* [79] by Heizer and Baumhoff depends heavily upon drawings.

The Far West

As used here this region includes Baja California, the coastal lowlands of California, Oregon, Washington, and British Columbia, and the panhandle of Alaska. The region is ecologically very diverse, varying from the temperate rain forests of the north through the Mediterranean environment of California to the peninsular desert of Baja California. However, its parts are united by their proximity to the Pacific and their separation from the rest of North America by rugged mountain ranges. Both Aikens [2] and Irwin [94] provide introductory chapters for the region from the perspective of the Great Basin, as I noted earlier in the Desert West section. Heizer's "The Western Coast of North America" [76] is a similar introduction but includes the Great Basin and assumes the perspective of California. Warren [183] gives us a general picture of the history of archaeological research in California. In contrast, Heizer's retrospective essay "Studying the Windmiller Culture" [77] provides some insight into the study of one particular central Californian prehistoric culture. Ascher's analysis of shell midden data [6] from the same general area is a useful case study for more advanced readers and an interesting contrast with similar investigations on the East Coast.

Heizer and Whipple's volume *The California Indians* [81] is a collection of previously published articles, of which six deal with prehistory. If read after the basic introductory works, each should be understandable to the beginner. As of this date, volume 8 of the *Handbook of North American Indians,* the California volume, is one of only two available [78]. Three of its articles deal with prehistory and a fourth deals with rock art. All are the most up-to-date summaries of California available to the general reader.

Unfortunately, for various reasons there are few regional summaries for the Far West. Baja California is poorly known, largely owing to a relative lack of research. California has for millennia been a complex cultural mosaic that defies coherent synthesis. The Northwest coast lacks prehistoric time depth and has yet to be investigated as fully as many other parts of North America.

North America's last prehistoric man was a California Indian of the Yahi tribe. He walked out of prehistory in 1911 and died at the University of California in 1916. The anthropologists who studied his culture knew him only as "Ishi." The reason we shall never know his real name and other fascinating details are contained in Theodora Kroeber's *Ishi in Two Worlds* [108], now in an extensively illustrated new edition. The same author's *Ishi, Last of His Tribe* [109] is a fictionalized account of his life in the wilderness. Both are excellent sources for beginners wishing to probe the humanistic side of modern research in prehistory.

Sprague's "The Pacific Northwest" [161] summarizes the history of research on the Northwest Coast, relatively little of which has been carried out north of Vancouver Island. Apart from Dumond's summary chapter "Alaska and the Northwest Coast" [37], there are no good introductory articles on Northwest prehistory, much less summary volumes. Indeed, most scholarly attention has tended to focus upon historic Indian art from this area. An example of this approach that goes beyond arty banalities is Holm's *Northwest Coast Indian Art: An Analysis of Form* [88]. Since historic Northwest Coast art has its roots in prehistory, Holm's comments are useful for understanding the stone sculptures shown in the 1975–76 exhibition. The sculptures are illustrated photographically in the exhibition catalog compiled and written by Wilson Duff [35].

Exploring Washington Archaeology [105] is an excellent introduction to the prehistory of one part of the Northwest Coast. It can serve most beginners as an introduction to the region as a whole. The book is short but contains many color photos and an excellent coverage of both archaeology and informative ethnographic comparisons.

As usual, rock art is treated separately from archaeology in the Far West. Crosby's *The Cave Paintings of Baja California* [28] is an amateurish but nicely illustrated survey of pictographs from that long peninsula. Heizer and Clewlow's two-volume *Prehistoric Rock Art of California* [80] gives up beauty for professional thoroughness in covering both pictographs and petroglyphs. Grant's *The Rock Paintings of the Chumash* [63] is a sober and well-illustrated treatment of the lavish pictographs around Santa Barbara, which the author reasonably links to Chumash ritual. Finally, *Indian Petroglyphs of the Pacific Northwest* [83] summarizes what is known of the prehistoric and historic rock art of that part of the Far West. Readers will probably note that it is no accident that engraved petroglyphs are the predominant form in the rainy Northwest while painted pictographs predominate in the dry caves of Baja California.

The Arctic and Subarctic

This vast wilderness is the largest of North America's archaeological regions and has been investigated by the smallest number of professional archaeologists. Studies here tend to fall into two groups: those having to do with the earliest migrations of people to the New World, which concentrate in Alaska and the Yukon, and those having to do with Eskimo prehistory. The latter are concerned with the past 5,000 years because of the relatively recent arrival of Eskimos and their cousins the Aleuts. Noble [134] and Dekin [32] provide us with brief histories of research in the Subarctic and the Arctic respectively. Beginners should read basic introductions before moving on to larger works. Collins's "The Arctic and Subarctic" [25] is the oldest of these but is still adequate. Campbell and Cordell's article with the same title [15] is newer and therefore includes more recent data. Probably the most up-to-date introduction can be gained by reading both Dumond's "Alaska and the Northwest Coast" [37] and Harp's "Pioneer Cultures of the Sub-Arctic and the Arctic" [72] in *Ancient Native Americans* [98].

Bandi's *Eskimo Prehistory* [9] is a good introduction

for beginning students, particularly in its largely descriptive middle chapters. Unfortunately it is burdened
with terminology borrowed rather inappropriately from
the Old World Upper Paleolithic and a rather old-
fashioned view of culture. I much prefer Dumond's *The
Eskimos and Aleuts* [36], which is recent and well illustrated and successfully links prehistoric sequences with
historic cultures and languages. This is easily the single
best source for the prehistory of this region.

Much of what we know of Arctic prehistory was
pioneered by J. L. Giddings. His work at Cape Denbigh
served as a foundation for both Eskimo prehistory and
Arctic archaeology. Although he initially misinterpreted
the age and significance of the data he recovered, these
problems were set right by the time he published *The
Archeology of Cape Denbigh* [57]. This was followed by
Ancient Men of the Arctic [58]. Although interpretations
and conclusions have changed in the years since their
publication, both books remain good reading.

At a more technical level we have Fitzhugh's edited
volume on maritime adaptations in the Arctic and Subarctic [47]. The papers in this book show current scientific trends in archaeological research in the region.
Students looking for something lighter in the way of
specialized Arctic research should read Anderson's
popular article on the Onion Portage site [3].

Collins *et al.* provide a very different approach to
the region in their book subtitled *2000 Years of American
Eskimo and Indian Art* [26]. The book is an exhibition
catalog of Eskimo, Athapascan, and Northwest Coast

art, some of it prehistoric. When used in conjunction with Dumond's book and introductory articles by Dumond [37] and Harp [72], the photos in this volume provide a very good illustrative supplement. I am particularly impressed by Collins's chapter on Eskimo art, which draws heavily upon his own excavations at sites of Old Bering Sea culture.

ALPHABETICAL LIST AND INDEX

*Denotes items suitable for secondary school students.

		Essay
Item		page
no.		no.

[1] Adams, Richard E. W. 1977. *Prehistoric Mesoamerica.* Boston: Little, Brown. (18)

[2]* Aikens, C. Melvin. 1978. "The Far West." In *Ancient Native Americans,* ed. Jesse D. Jennings, pp. 131–81. See [98]. (34, 37)

[3] Anderson, Douglas D. 1968. "A Stone Age Campsite at the Gateway to America." *Scientific American* 218(6):24–33. See [123], pp. 29–38; [204], pp. 61–70. (41)

[4] Armillas, Pedro. 1964. "Northern Mesoamerica." In *Prehistoric Man in the New World,* ed. Jesse D. Jennings and Edward Norbeck, pp. 291–329. See [100]. (18)

[5] Asch, David L. 1976. *The Middle Woodland Population of the Lower Illinois Valley: A Study in Paleodemographic Methods.*

Evanston, Ill.: Northwestern University Archaeological Program.   (27)

[6]   Ascher, Robert. 1959. "A Prehistoric Population Estimate Using Midden Analysis and Two Population Models." *Southwestern Journal of Anthropology* 15(2):168–78. See [65], pp. 340–44.   (37)

[7]   Aveni, Anthony F., ed. 1975. *Archaeoastronomy in Pre-Columbian America*. Austin: University of Texas Press.   (17)

[8]   ———. 1977. *Native American Astronomy*. Austin: University of Texas Press.   (17)

[9]   Bandi, Hans-Georg. 1969. *Eskimo Prehistory*. College, Alaska: University of Alaska Press (distributed by University of Washington Press). Originally published in German, 1964.   (40)

[10]   Bannister, Bryant. 1962. "The Interpretation of Tree-Ring Dates." *American Antiquity* 27(4):508–14. See [65], pp. 159–64.   (35)

[11]*   Brain, Jeffery P., Peter Copeland, Louis de la Haba, Mary Ann Harrell, Tee Loftin, Jay Luvaas, and Douglas W.

Schwartz. 1976. *Clues to America's Past.* Washington, D.C.: National Geographic Society.   (8)

[12]*   Brennan, Louis A. 1975. *Artifacts of Prehistoric America.* Harrisburg: Stackpole.   (23)

[13]   Brose, David S. 1973. "The Northeastern United States." in *The Development of North American Archaeology,* ed. James E. Fitting, pp. 84–115. See [46].   (23)

[14]   Buikstra, Jane E. 1976. *Hopewell in the Lower Illinois Valley: A Regional Approach to the Study of Human Biological Variability and Prehistoric Behavior.* Evanston, Ill.: Northwestern Archaeological Program.   (27)

[15]   Campbell, John M., and Linda Seinfeld Cordell. 1975. "The Arctic and Subarctic." In *North America,* ed. Shirley Gorenstein, pp. 36–73. See [61].   (40)

[16]*   Casson, Lionel. 1972. "Who Got Here First?" *Horizon* 14(2):96–103. See [42], pp. 262–72.   (16)

[17]*   ———. 1975. "The Lure of the Vikings." *Horizon* 17(2):64–79.   (16)

[18]*   ———. 1977. "Who First Crossed the
         Oceans?" In *Mysteries of the Past,* ed.
         Joseph J. Thorndike, Jr., pp. 8–31. New
         York: American Heritage.   (16)

[19]   Chapman, Carl H. 1975. *The Archaeology
         of Missouri,* vol. 1. Columbia: University
         of Missouri Press.   (33)

[20]   Chard, Chester. 1969. *Man in Prehistory.*
         New York: McGraw-Hill.   (9)

[21]*   Claiborne, Robert. 1973. *The First Ameri-
         cans.* New York: Time-Life.   (12)

[22]*   Coe, Michael D. 1964. "The Chinampas
         of Mexico." *Scientific American*
         211(1):90–98. See [204], pp. 231–39.   (19)

[23]*   ———. 1971. "The Shadow of the Ol-
         mecs." *Horizon* 13(4):66–74. See [42],
         pp. 272–83.   (18)

[24]*   Coe, Ralph T. 1977. *Sacred Circles: Two
         Thousand Years of North American Indian
         Art.* Kansas City: Nelson Gallery of Art.
         Reprinted, Seattle: University of Wash-
         ington Press, 1977.   (14)

[25]* Collins, Henry B. 1964. "The Arctic and Subarctic." In *Prehistoric Man in the New World*, ed. Jesse D. Jennings and Edward Norbeck, pp. 85–114. See [100]. (40)

[26] Collins, Henry B., Frederica De Laguna, Edward Carpenter, and Peter Stone. 1973. *The Far North: 2000 Years of American Eskimo and Indian Art*. Washington, D.C.: National Gallery of Art. Reprinted, Bloomington: Indiana University Press, 1977. (41)

[27] Corliss, William R., ed. 1974. *Strange Artifacts: A Sourcebook on Ancient Man*. Glen Arm, Md.: Corliss. (7)

[28]* Crosby, Harry. 1975. *The Cave Paintings of Baja California: The Great Murals of an Unknown People*. La Jolla, Ca.: Copley Press. (39)

[29]* Culbert, T. Patrick. 1978. "Mesoamerica." In *Ancient Native Americans*, ed. Jesse D. Jennings, pp. 403–53. See [98]. (18)

[30] Deetz, James. 1965. *The Dynamics of Stylistic Change in Arikara Ceramics*. Illinois Studies in Anthropology no. 4. Urbana: University of Illinois Press. (32)

[31]*   ———. 1967. *Invitation to Archaeology.*
Garden City, N.Y.: Natural History
Press.   (2)

[32]   Dekin, Albert A., Jr. 1973. "The Arctic."
In *The Development of North American Archaeology,* ed. James E. Fitting, pp.
15–48. See [46].   (40)

[33]   Dickens, Roy S., Jr. 1976. *Cherokee
Prehistory: The Pisgah Phase in the Appalachian Summit Region.* Knoxville: University of Tennessee Press.   (30)

[34]   Dragoo, Don W. 1963. *Mounds for the
Dead: An Analysis of the Adena Culture.
Annals* of the Carnegie Museum, vol. 37.
Pittsburgh: Carnegie Museum.   (27)

[35]   Duff, Wilson. 1975. *Images: Stone: B.C.:
Thirty Centuries of Northwest Coast Indian
Sculpture.* Seattle: University of Washington Press.   (39)

[36]   Dumond, Don E. 1977. *The Eskimos and
Aleuts.* London: Thames and Hudson.   (41)

[37]*   ———. 1978. "Alaska and the Northwest Coast." In *Ancient Native Americans,*

ed. Jesse D. Jennings, pp. 43–93. See
[98]. (38, 40, 42)

[38]* Easby, Dudley T., Jr. 1966. "Early
Metallurgy in the New World." *Scientific
American* 214(4):72–81. See [204], pp.
249–56. (28)

[39]* Ebert, James I., and Robert K. Hitch-
cock. 1975. "Chaco Canyon's Mysterious
Highways." *Horizon* 17(4): 48–53. (35)

[40]* Ekholm, Gordon F. 1964. "Transpacific
Contacts." In *Prehistoric Man in the New
World,* ed. Jesse D. Jennings and Edward
Norbeck, pp. 489–510. See [100]. (16)

[41]* Fagan, Brian M. 1972. *In the Beginning:
An Introduction to Archaeology.* Boston:
Little, Brown. Revised ed., 1978. (3)

[42]* ———., ed. 1974. *Corridors in Time: A
Reader in Introductory Archaeology.* Boston: Little, Brown. (6)

[43]* ———. 1977. "Who Were the Mound
Builders?" In *Mysteries of the Past,* ed.
Joseph J. Thorndike, Jr., pp. 118–35.
New York: American Heritage. (28)

[44]*   ———. 1978. *Archaeology: A Brief Intro-*
duction. Boston: Little, Brown.   (3)

[45]   Fitting, James E. 1970. *The Archaeology of*
Michigan: A Guide to the Prehistory of the
Great Lakes Region. Garden City, N.Y.:
Natural History Press.   (26)

[46]   ———, ed. 1973. *The Development of*
North American Archaeology: Essays in the
History of Regional Traditions. Garden
City, N.Y.: Doubleday Anchor.   (4)

[47]   Fitzhugh, William, ed. 1975. *Prehistoric*
Maritime Adaptations of the Circumpolar
Zone. Chicago: Aldine.   (41)

[48]*   Folsom, Franklin. 1971. *America's An-*
cient Treasures: Guide to Archaeological
Sites and Museums. New York: Rand
McNally.   (xi, 13)

[49]   Forbis, Richard G. 1975. "Eastern North
America." In *North America,* ed. Shirley
Gorenstein, pp. 74–102. See [61].   (23)

[50]*   ———. 1975. "The Paleoamericans." In
North America, ed. Shirley Gorenstein,
pp. 17–35. See [61].   (19)

[51]* Fowler, Melvin L. 1975. "A Pre-
Columbian Urban Center on the Mississippi." *Scientific American* 233(2):92–
101. (Available as an offprint.) (30)

[52] Frison, George C. 1973. "The Plains." In
*The Development of North American Ar-
chaeology*, ed. James E. Fitting, pp.
151–84. See [46]. (31)

[53] ———, ed. 1974. *The Casper Site: A Hell
Gap Bison Kill on the High Plains.* New
York: Academic Press. (21)

[54] ———. 1978. *Prehistoric Hunters of the
High Plains.* New York: Academic Press. (31)

[55]* Fundaburk, Emma Lila, and Mary
Douglass Foreman, eds. 1957. *Sun Cir-
cles and Human Hands; The Southeastern
Indians—Art and Industry.* Luverne, Ala.:
Emma Lila Fundaburk. (30)

[56]* Garbarino, Merwyn S. 1976. *Native
American Heritage.* Boston: Little,
Brown. (13)

[57] Giddings, J. L. 1964. *The Archeology of
Cape Denbigh.* Providence: Brown University Press. (41)

[58]*   ———. 1967. *Ancient Men of the Arctic.*
New York: Knopf.   (41)

[59]   Gilliland, Marion Spjut. 1965. *The Ma-
terial Culture of Key Marco Florida.*
Gainesville: University Presses of
Florida. New expanded ed., 1975.   (31)

[60]   Gladwin, Harold S. 1957. *A History of the
Ancient Southwest.* Portland, Me.: Bond
Wheelwright.   (35)

[61]*   Gorenstein, Shirley, ed. 1975. *North
America.* New York: St. Martin's Press.   (11)

[62]   Gradwohl, David M. 1969. *Prehistoric
Villages in Eastern Nebraska.* Nebraska
State Historical Society Publications in
Anthropology, 4. Lincoln: Nebraska
State Historical Society.   (32)

[63]*   Grant, Campbell. 1965. *The Rock Paint-
ings of the Chumash: A Study of a California
Indian Culture.* Berkeley: University of
California Press.   (39)

[64]*   ———. 1967. *Rock Art of the American
Indian.* New York: Crowell.   (14)

[65]   Green, Ernestene L., ed. 1973. *In Search
        of Man: Readings in Archaeology.* Boston:
        Little, Brown.   (6)

[66]*   Griffin, James B. 1964. "The Northeast
        Woodlands Area." In *Prehistoric Man in
        the New World,* ed. Jesse D. Jennings and
        Edward Norbeck, pp. 223–58. See
        [100].   (23)

[67]   ———. 1967. "Eastern North American
        Archaeology: A Summary." *Science*
        156(3772):175–91.   (23)

[68]*   ———. 1978. "The Midlands and
        Northeastern United States." In *Ancient
        Native Americans,* ed. Jesse D. Jennings,
        pp. 221–79. See [98].   (23)

[69]*   Haag, William G. 1962. "The Bering
        Strait Land Bridge." *Scientific American*
        206(1):112–23. See [123], pp. 11–18;
        [204], pp. 263–70.   (20)

[70]   ———. 1974. "The Adena Culture." In
        Archaeological Researches in Retrospect, ed.
        Gordon R. Willey, pp. 119–45. See
        [196].   (27)

[71]   Haines, Francis. 1976. *The Plains In-dians: Their Origins, Migrations, and Cul-tural Development.* New York: Crowell.   (33)

[72]*   Harp, Elmer, Jr. 1978. "Pioneer Cul-tures of the Sub-Arctic and the Arctic." In *Ancient Native Americans,* ed. Jesse D. Jennings, pp. 95–129. See [98].   (42)

[73]   Haury, Emil W. 1958. "Evidence at Point of Pines for a Prehistoric Migra-tion from Northern Arizona." In *Migra-tions in New World Culture History,* ed. Raymond H. Thompson, pp. 1–8. Tuc-son: University of Arizona Bulletin 27, vol. 29, no. 2. See [65], pp. 381–88.   (36)

[74]   ———. 1976. *The Hohokam, Desert Farm-ers and Craftmen: Excavations at Snaketown, 1964–65.* Tucson: University of Arizona Press.   (36)

[75]   Haynes, C. Vance, Jr. 1966. "Elephant-Hunting in North America." *Scientific American* 214(6):104–12. See [123], pp. 44–52; [204], pp. 204–12.   (20)

[76]   Heizer, Robert F. 1964. "The Western Coast of North America." In *Prehistoric Man in the New World,* ed. Jesse D.

Jennings and Edward Norbeck, pp.
117–48. See [100]. (37)

[77] ———. 1974. "Studying the Windmiller
Culture." In *Archaeological Researches in
Retrospect*, ed. Gordon R. Willey, pp.
179–204. See [196]. (37)

[78] ———. ed. 1978. *Handbook of North
American Indians.* William C. Sturtevant,
gen. ed. Vol. 8. *California.* Washington,
D.C.: Smithsonian Institution. (15, 38)

[79] Heizer, Robert F., and Martin A.
Baumhoff. 1962. *Prehistoric Rock Art of
Nevada and Eastern California.* Berkeley:
University of California Press. New ed.,
1975. (36)

[80] Heizer, Robert F., and C. W. Clewlow,
Jr. 1973. *Prehistoric Rock Art of California.*
2 vols. Ramona, Calif.: Ballena. (39)

[81] Heizer, Robert F., and M. A. Whipple.
1965. *The California Indians; A Source
Book.* Berkeley: University of California
Press. Revised and enlarged ed., 1971. (37)

[82]   Hester, James J. 1976. *Introduction to Archaeology*. New York: Holt, Rinehart and
Winston.   (9)

[83]   Hill, Beth, and Ray Hill. 1975. *Indian
Petroglyphs of the Pacific Northwest*. Seattle: University of Washington Press.   (39)

[84]   Hill, James, N. 1967. "The Problem of
Sampling." In *Chapters in the Prehistory of
Eastern Arizona*, vol. 3. *Fieldiana: Anthropology* 57:145–57. See [65], pp.
60–73.   (36)

[85]   Hlady, Walter M., ed. 1970. *Ten
Thousand Years: Archaeology in Manitoba*.
Altona, Canada: D. W. Friesen.   (29)

[86]*   Hole, Frank, and Robert F. Heizer.
1965. *An Introduction to Prehistoric Archeology*. New York: Holt, Rinehart and
Winston. 3d. ed, 1973.   (3)

[87]*   ———. 1977. *Prehistoric Archeology: A
Brief Introduction*. New York: Holt,
Rinehart and Winston.   (3)

[88]   Holm, Bill. 1965. *Northwest Coast Indian
Art: An Analysis of Form*. Seattle: University of Washington Press.   (39)

[89]   Houart, Gail L. 1971. *Koster: A Stratified Archaic Site in the Lower Illinois Valley.* Illinois State Museum Reports of Investigations no. 22. Springfield: Illinois State Museum.   (27)

[90]   Hudson, Charles. 1976. *The Southeastern Indians.* Knoxville: University of Tennessee Press.   (30)

[91]*   Hume, Ivor Noël. 1969. *Historical Archaeology.* New York: Knopf. Reprinted, New York: Norton, 1975.   (8)

[92]   ———. 1970. *A Guide to the Artifacts of Colonial America.* New York: Knopf.   (8)

[93]   Ingstad, Anne Stine. 1977. *The Discovery of a Norse Settlement in America.* Oslo: Universitetsforlaget; New York: Columbia University Press.   (16)

[94]   Irwin, Henry T. 1975. "The Far West." In *North America,* ed. Shirley Gorenstein, pp. 133–64. See [61].   (34, 37)

[95]   Jennings, Jesse D. 1957. *Danger Cave.* University of Utah Anthropological Papers, no. 27. Salt Lake City: University of Utah Press. See [65], pp. 108–17. Also

published as Society for American Archaeology, *Memoir* no. 14. Washington, D.C.: Society for American Archaeology, 1957.   (34)

[96]*   ———. 1964. "The Desert West." In *Prehistoric Man in the New World,* ed. Jesse D. Jennings and Edward Norbeck, pp. 149–74. See [100].   (34)

[97]   ———. 1968. *Prehistory of North America.* New York: McGraw-Hill. New ed., 1974.   (12)

[98]*   ———, ed. 1978. *Ancient Native Americans.* San Francisco: Freeman.   (10, 12)

[99]*   ———. 1978. "Origins." In *Ancient Native Americans,* ed. Jesse D. Jennings, pp. 1–41. See [98].   (19)

[100]   Jennings, Jesse D., and Edward Norbeck, eds. 1964. *Prehistoric Man in the New World.* Published for William Marsh Rice University. Chicago: University of Chicago Press. 3d. ed., 1974.   (10)

[101]*   Jett, Stephen C. 1978. "Pre-Columbian Transoceanic Contacts." In *Ancient Native Americans,* ed. Jesse D. Jennings, pp. 593–650. See [98].   (16)

[102]   Johnson, Eldon. 1969. *The Prehistoric
         Peoples of Minnesota.* Saint Paul: Min-
         nesota Historical Society. Revised ed.,
         1978.   (26)

[103]   Keel, Bennie C. 1976. *Cherokee Archaeol-
         ogy: A Study of the Appalachian Summit.*
         Knoxville: University of Tennessee
         Press.   (30)

[104]   Kent, Barry C., Ira F. Smith, III, and
         Catherine McCann, eds. 1971. *Founda-
         tions of Pennsylvania Prehistory.* Pennsyl-
         vania Historical and Museum Commis-
         sion Anthropological Series, no. 1.
         Harrisburg: Pennsylvania Historical
         and Museum Commission.   (25)

[105]   Kirk, Ruth, and Richard D. Daugherty.
         1978. *Exploring Washington Archaeology.*
         Seattle: University of Washington Press. (39)

[106]   Knudson, S. J. 1978. *Culture in Retros-
         pect: An Introduction to Archaeology.*
         Chicago: Rand McNally.   (3)

[107]   Kraft, Herbert C., ed. 1974. *A Delaware
         Indian Symposium.* Pennsylvania Histori-
         cal and Museum Commission An-
         thropological Series, no. 4. Harrisburg:

Pennsylvania Historical and Museum
Commission.   (25)

[108]*   Kroeber, Theodora. 1961. *Ishi in Two
Worlds: A Biography of the Last Wild Indian
in North America.* Berkeley: University of
California Press. New illustrated ed.,
1976.   (38)

[109]*   ———. 1964. *Ishi, Last of His Tribe.* New
York: Bantam.   (38)

[110]   Krupp, E. C., ed. 1977. *In Search of Ancient Astronomies.* New York: Doubleday.   (17)

[111]   Larson, Lewis H., Jr. 1971. "Archaeological Implications of Social Stratification at the Etowah Site, Georgia." In
*Approaches to the Social Dimensions of Mor-
tuary Practices,* James A. Brown, ed. Society for American Archaeology, *Memoir*
no. 25. Washington, D.C.: Society for
American Archaeology, pp. 58–67. See
[65], pp. 269–82.   (30)

[112]   Lehmer, Donald J. 1971. *Introduction to
Middle Missouri Archeology.* Anthropological Papers, no. 1. National Park Service.
Washington, D.C.: Government Print-
ing Office.   (32)

[113]   Lewis, Cara L. 1971. *A Handbook for Delmarva Archaeology.* Dover: Office of Archaeology, State of Delaware.   (25)

[114]* Lipe, William D. 1978. "The Southwest." In *Ancient Native Americans,* ed. Jesse D. Jennings, pp. 327–401. See [98].   (34)

[115]   Longacre, William A. 1964. "Sociological Implications of the Ceramic Analysis." In *Chapters in the Prehistory of Eastern Arizona,* vol. 2. *Fieldiana: Anthropology* 53:155–67. See [65], pp. 202–12.   (36)

[116]   Longacre, William A., and James E. Ayres. 1968. "Archeological Lessons from an Apache Wickiup." In *New Perspectives in Archeology,* ed. Sally R. Binford and Lewis R. Binford. Chicago: Aldine, pp. 151–59. See [65], pp. 321–29.   (36)

[117]* McGregor, John C. 1941. *Southwestern Archaeology.* New York: John Wiley. Reprinted, Urbana: University of Illinois Press, 1965.   (35)

[118]   McKusick, Marshall. 1964. *Men of Ancient Iowa, as Revealed by Archeological*

Discoveries. Ames: Iowa State University Press. (33)

[119] ———. 1970. *The Davenport Conspiracy.* Iowa City: State Archaeologist. Distributed by University of Iowa Press. (7)

[120]* MacNeish, Richard S. 1964. "The Origins of New World Civilization." *Scientific American* 211(5):29–37. See [123], pp. 155–63. (18)

[121] ———. 1971. "Early Man in the Andes." *Scientific American* 224(4):36–46. See [123], pp. 69–79; [204], pp. 143–53. (20)

[122]* ———. 1971. "Speculation about How and Why Food Production and Village Life Developed in the Tehuacan Valley, Mexico." *Archaeology* 24(4):307–15. See [42], pp. 209–22. (18)

[123] ———, ed. 1973. *Early Man in America.* San Francisco: W. H. Freeman. (20)

[124] ———. 1978. *The Science of Archaeology?* North Scituate, Mass.: Duxbury Press. (5)

[125] Magnusson, Magnus. 1973. *Viking Expansion Westwards.* New York: Henry Z. Walck. (16)

[126]   Marek, Kurt W. 1971. *The First Americans: A Story of North American Archaeology*, by C. W. Ceram [pseud.]. New York: Harcourt Brace Jovanovich.   (5)

[127]   Martin, Paul S. 1974. "Early Development in Mogollon Research." In *Archaeological Researches in Retrospect*, ed. Gordon R. Willey, pp. 3–29. See [196].   (34)

[128]   Martin, Paul S., and Fred Plog. 1973. *The Archaeology of Arizona: A Study of the Southwest Region*. Garden City, N.Y.: Natural History Press.   (35)

[129]* Meggers, Betty J. 1972. *Prehistoric America*. Chicago: Aldine.   (10)

[130]   Meggers, Betty J., and Clifford Evans. 1966. "A Transpacific Contact in 3000 B.C." *Scientific American* 214(1):28–35. See [204], pp. 97–104.   (16)

[131]   Miles, Charles. 1963. *Indian and Eskimo Artifacts of North America*. New York: Bonanza Books.   (14)

[132]* Millon, Rene. 1967. "Teotihuacan." *Scientific American* 216(6): 38–48. See [204], pp. 115–25.   (19)

[133]   Muller, Jon D. 1978. "The Southeast."
         In *Ancient Native Americans,* ed. Jesse D.
         Jennings, pp. 281–325. See [98].   (23, 29)

[134]   Noble, William C. 1973. "Canada." In
         The Development of North American Ar-
         chaeology, ed. James E. Fitting, pp.
         49–83. See [46].   (40)

[135]*   Ogburn, Charlton, Jr. 1970. "The First
         Discovery of America." *Horizon* 12(1):
         92–99. See [42], pp. 175–85.   (20)

[136]   Pendergast, James F., and Bruce G.
         Trigger. 1972. *Cartier's Hochelaga and the*
         Dawson Site. Montreal: McGill-Queen's
         University Press.   (25)

[137]*   Pfeiffer, John. 1974. "America's First
         City." *Horizon* 16(2):58–63.   (30)

[138]*   ———. 1975. "The Life and Death of a
         Great City." *Horizon* 17(1):82–95.   (19)

[139]*   Potter, Martha A. 1968. *Ohio's Prehistoric*
         Peoples. Columbus: Ohio Historical
         Society.   (27)

[140]   Prufer, Olaf H. 1964. "The Hopewell
         Cult." *Scientific American* 211(6):90–102.
         See [204], pp. 222–30.   (28)

[141]   Quimby, George I. 1960. *Indian Life in the Upper Great Lakes, 11,000 B.C. to A.D. 1800*. Chicago: University of Chicago Press. New ed., 1971.   (26)

[142]   ———. 1966. *Indian Culture and European Trade Goods*. Madison: University of Wisconsin Press. Reprinted, Westport, Conn.: Greenwood, 1978.   (26)

[143]* Reed, Erik K. 1964. "The Greater Southwest." In *Prehistoric Man in the New World,* ed. Jesse D. Jennings and Edward Norbeck, pp. 175–91. See [100].   (34)

[144]   Ritchie, William A. 1965. *The Archaeology of New York State*. Garden City, N.Y.: Natural History Press. Revised ed., 1969.   (24)

[145]   ———. 1969. *The Archaeology of Martha's Vineyard: a Framework for the Prehistory of Southern New England*. Garden City, N.Y.: Natural History Press.   (24)

[146]   Ritchie, William A., and Robert E. Funk. 1973. *Aboriginal Settlement Patterns in the Northeast*. New York State Museum and Science Service, *Memoir* no. 20. Albany: University of the State of New York.   (24)

[147]*   Ritzenthaler, Robert E. 1953. *Prehistoric Indians of Wisconsin.* Milwaukee Public Museum, Popular Science Handbook Series, no. 4. Milwaukee: Milwaukee Public Museum. Reprinted, 1970.   (26)

[148]   Rohn, Arthur H. 1973. "The Southwest and Intermontane West." In *The Development of North American Archaeology,* ed. James E. Fitting, pp. 185–211. See [46].   (34)

[149]   Rouse, Irving. 1972. *Introduction to Prehistory: A Systematic Approach.* New York: McGraw-Hill.   (3)

[150]   Salwen, Bert. 1962. "Sea Levels and Archaeology in the Long Island Sound Area." *American Antiquity* 28(1):46–55. See [65], pp. 149–58.   (25)

[151]   Sanders, William T., and Joseph Marino. 1970. *New World Prehistory: Archaeology of the American Indian.* Englewood Cliffs, N.J.: Prentice-Hall.   (10)

[152]   Schaafsma, Polly. 1971. *The Rock Art of Utah: A Study from the Donald Scott Collection.* Papers of the Peabody Museum of Archaeology and Ethnology, vol. 65.

Cambridge: Harvard University, Peabody Museum. (36)

[153] ———. 1975. *Rock Art in New Mexico.* Albuquerque: University of New Mexico Press. (36)

[154]* Sears, William H. 1964. "The Southeastern United States." In *Prehistoric Man in the New World,* ed. Jesse D. Jennings and Edward Norbeck, pp. 259–87. See [100]. (23, 29)

[155]* Silverberg, Robert. 1968. *Mound Builders of Ancient America: The Archaeology of a Myth.* Greenwich, Conn.: New York Graphic Society. Reprinted, New York: Ballantine, 1974. (7)

[156] Simmons, William S. 1970. *Cautantowwit's House: An Indian Burial Ground on the Island of Conanicut in Narragansett Bay.* Providence: Brown University Press. (25)

[157] Smith, Jason W. 1976. *Foundations of Archaeology.* Beverly Hills, Calif.: Glencoe. (3)

[158]* Snow, Dean R. 1976. *The Archaeology of North America.* New York: Viking. (12)

[159]   ———. 1977. "Rock Art and the Power of Shamans." *Natural History* 86(2):42–49.   (28)

[160]   Spencer, Robert F., Jesse D. Jennings, *et al.* 1977. *The Native Americans: Ethnology and Backgrounds of the North American Indians.* New York: Harper and Row. Originally published as *The Native Americans: Prehistory and Ethnology of the North American Indians.* New York: Harper and Row, 1965.   (13)

[161]   Sprague, Roderick. 1973. "The Pacific Northwest." In *The Development of North American Archaeology,* ed. James E. Fitting, pp. 250–85. See [46].   (38)

[162]   Stoltman, James B. 1973. "The Southeastern United States." In *The Development of North American Archaeology,* ed. James E. Fitting, pp. 116–50. See [46].   (23)

[163]   Struever, Stuart. 1968. "Woodland Subsistence-Settlement Systems in the Lower Illinois Valley." In *New Perspectives in Archeology,* ed. Sally R. Binford and Lewis R. Binford. Chicago: Aldine, pp. 285–312. See [42], pp. 223–31.   (26)

[164]　Struever, Stuart and Felicia Antonelli
Holton. 1979. *Koster: Americans in Search
of Their Prehistoric Past.* Garden City,
N.Y.: Anchor.　　　　　　　　　　　　(26)

[165]*　Stuart, George E., and Gene S. Stuart.
1969. *Discovering Man's Past in the
Americas.* Washington, D.C.: National
Geographic Society.　　　　　　　　　　(10)

[166]　Swadesh, Morris. 1964. "Linguistic
Overview." In *Prehistoric Man in the New
World,* ed. Jesse D. Jennings and Edward
Norbeck, pp. 527–56. See [100].　　　　(17)

[167]　Swartz, B. K., Jr., ed. 1971. *Adena: The
Seeking of an Identity.* Muncie, Ind.: Ball
State University.　　　　　　　　　　　(27)

[168]　———. 1973. *Indiana's Prehistoric Past.*
Muncie, Ind.: Ball State University.　　(27)

[169]　Swauger, James L. 1974. *Rock Art of the
Upper Ohio Valley.* Graz: Akademische
Druck-und. Verlagsanstalt.　　　　　　(28)

[170]　Tamarin, Alfred, and Shirley Glubok.
1975. *Ancient Indians of the Southwest.*
Garden City New York: Doubleday.　　(35)

[171]   Taylor, Walter W. 1967. *A Study of Archeology.* Carbondale: Southern Illinois University Press.   (6)

[172]   Teel, William. 1976. *An Outline of Pre-Columbian and American Indian Art.* Winchester, Mass.: University Prints.   (14)

[173]*   Thomas, David H. 1974. *Predicting the Past: An Introduction to Anthropological Archaeology.* New York: Holt, Rinehart and Winston.   (3)

[174]   Tolstoy, Paul. 1975. "From the Old World to the New World via Bering Strait." In *North America,* ed. Shirley Gorenstein, pp. 165–85. See [61].   (21)

[175]   Trigger, Bruce G., ed. 1978. *Handbook of North American Indians.* William C. Sturtevant, gen. ed. Vol. 15. *Northeast.* Washington, D.C.: Smithsonian Institution.   (15, 24)

[176]   Tuck, James A. 1970. "An Archaic Indian Cemetery in Newfoundland." *Scientific American* 222(6):112–21. See [204], pp. 105–14.   (29)

[177]   ———. 1971. "The Iroquois Confederacy." *Scientific American* 224(2):32–42. See [204], pp. 190–200.   (24)

[178]   ———. 1971. *Onondaga Iroquois Prehistory: A Study in Settlement Archaeology.* Syracuse: Syracuse University Press.   (24)

[179]   Tuck, James A., and Robert J. McGhee. 1976. "An Archaic Indian Burial Mound in Labrador." *Scientific American* 235(5):122–29.   (29)

[180]   Turnbaugh, William A. 1975. *Man, Land, and Time: The Cultural Prehistory and Demographic Patterns of North-Central Pennsylvania.* Evansville, Ind.: Unigraphic.   (25)

[181]   Vastokas, Joan M., and Romas K. Vastokas. 1973. *Sacred Art of the Algonkians: a Study of the Peterborough Petroglyphs.* Peterborough, Ont.: Mansard Press.   (28)

[182]*   Walthall, John A. 1977. *Moundville: An Introduction to the Archaeology of a Mississippian Chiefdom.* Tuscaloosa: Alabama Museum of Natural History.   (30)

[183]   Warren, Claude N. 1973. "California." In *The Development of North American Archaeology,* ed. James E. Fitting, pp. 212–49. See [46].   (37)

[184]   Washburn, Dorothy K. 1975. "The
American Southwest." In *North America*,
ed. Shirley Gorenstein, pp. 103–32. See
[61].   (34)

[185]*   Wauchope, Robert. 1962. *Lost Tribes and
Sunken Continents; Myth and Method in the
Study of American Indians*. Chicago: Uni-
versity of Chicago Press.   (7)

[186]   Weaver, Muriel Porter. 1972. *The Aztecs,
Maya, and Their Predecessors: Archaeology
of Mesoamerica*. New York: Seminar
Press.   (18)

[187]   Webb, William S. 1946. *Indian Knoll*.
University of Kentucky Reports in Anthropology and Archaeology, 4 (3), part
1. Lexington: University of Kentucky
Press. New ed., Knoxville: Uni-
versity of Tennessee Press, 1974.   (27)

[188]   Webb, William S., and Raymond S.
Baby. 1957. *The Adena People No. 2*. Columbus: Ohio Historical Society.   (27)

[189]   Webb, William S., and Charles E. Snow.
1945. *The Adena People*. University of
Kentucky Department of Anthropology
Publications, 6. Lexington: University of

Kentucky. New ed., Knoxville: University of Tennessee Press, 1974. (27)

[190]* Wedel, Waldo R. 1964. "The Great Plains." In *Prehistoric Man in the New World,* ed. Jesse D. Jennings and Edward Norbeck, pp. 193–220. See [100]. (31)

[191]* ———. 1978. "The Prehistoric Plains." In *Ancient Native Americans,* ed. Jesse D. Jennings, pp. 183–219. See [98]. (31)

[192] Weslager, Clinton A., 1944. *Delaware's Buried Past: A Story of Archeological Adventure.* Philadelphia: University of Pennsylvania Press. New ed., New Brunswick: Rutgers University Press, 1968. (25)

[193]* Wheat, Joe Ben. 1967. "A Paleo-Indian Bison Kill." *Scientific American* 216(1):44–52. See [123], pp. 80–88; [204], pp. 213–21. (20)

[194] ———. 1972. *The Olsen-Chubbuck Site: A Paleo-Indian Bison Kill.* Society for American Archaeology, *Memoir* no. 26. Washington, D.C.: Society for American Archaeology. See [42], pp. 154–74; [65], pp. 87–107. (20)

[195]   Willey, Gordon R. 1966. *An Introduction to American Archaeology.* Vol. 1. *North and Middle America.* Englewood Cliffs, N.J.: Prentice-Hall.   (11, 29)

[196]   ———, ed. 1974. *Archaeological Researches in Retrospect.* Cambridge, Mass.: Winthrop Publishers.   (4)

[197]   Willey, Gordon R., and Jeremy A. Sabloff. 1974. *A History of American Archaeology.* San Francisco: Freeman.   (4)

[198]   Wilmsen, Edwin N. 1974. *Lindenmeier: A Pleistocene Hunting Society.* New York: Harper and Row.   (21)

[199]   Wilson, David. 1975. *The New Archaeology.* New York: Knopf.   (6)

[200]   Wood, W. Raymond. 1976. *Prehistoric Man and His Environments: A Case Study in the Ozark Highland.* New York: Academic Press.   (33)

[201]   Woodall, J. Ned. 1972. *An Introduction to Modern Archaeology.* Cambridge, Mass.: Schenkman (distributed by General Learning Press).   (4)

[202]   Wormington, Hannah M. 1947. *Prehis-
         toric Indians of the Southwest.* Denver:
         Colorado Museum of Natural History
         Popular Series no. 7. Denvèr: Denver
         Museum of Natural History. Reprinted,
         1973.   (35)

[203]   Wright, James V. 1972. *Ontario Prehis-
         tory: An Eleven-Thousand-Year Archaeolog-
         ical Outline.* Ottawa: National Museums
         of Canada.   (29)

[204]*   Zubrow, Ezra B. W., Margaret C. Fritz,
         and John M. Fritz. 1974. *New World
         Archaeology: Theoretical and Cultural
         Transformations; Readings from Scientific
         American.* San Francisco: Freeman.   (11, 20)

The Newberry Library
Center for the History of the American Indian
Founding Director: D'Arcy McNickle
Director: Francis Jennings

Established in 1972 by the Newberry Library, in conjunction with the Committee on Institutional Cooperation of eleven midwestern universities, the Center makes the resources of one of America's foremost research libraries in the Humanities available to those interested in improving the quality and effectiveness of teaching American Indian history. The Newberry's collections include some 100,000 volumes on the history of the American Indian and offer specialized resources for studying historical aspects of Indian-White relations and Indian linguistics. The Center also assists Native Americans engaged in writing tribal histories and developing educational materials.

ADVISORY COMMITTEE

Chairman: Alfonso Ortiz
University of New Mexico

Robert F. Berkhofer
University of Michigan

Robert V. Dumont, Jr.
Native American Educational
Services/Antioch College;
Fort Peck Reservation

Raymond D. Fogelson
University of Chicago

William T. Hagan
State University of New
York College, Fredonia

Nancy O. Lurie
Milwaukee Public Museum

Cheryl Metoyer-Duran
University of California,
Los Angeles

N. Scott Momaday
Stanford University

Father Peter J. Powell
St. Augustine Indian Center

Father Paul Prucha, s.j.
Marquette University

Faith Smith
Native American Educational
Services/Antioch College;
Chicago

Sol Tax
University of Chicago

Robert K. Thomas
Wayne State University

Robert M. Utley
Advisory Council on Historical
Preservation; Washington, D.C.

Antoinette McNickle Vogel
Gaithersburg, MD.

Dave Warren
Institute of American Indian Arts

Wilcomb E. Washburn
Smithsonian Institution

DATE DUE

DEC 14. 1994			
APR 1 5			
GAYLORD			PRINTED IN U.S.A.